1

Dedication

To the animates, peoples and animals diseased, deceased, devastated, dispossessed, displaced due to mankind's personal, social and cultural contemporary trends; and global political, ideological, conflicts; and/or natural cataclysms.

Disclaimer

In addition to empirical observation the material for the construction of treatise on the 'Cotemporary Trends', has been gleaned from, published studies, documentaries print and/or broadcast media reports.

The author presumes, perhaps naively, that the published studies, documentaries and print, broadcast media reports are public intellectual property; and that the references, comments, quotes and stats therein are authentic, objective and veritable.

It is author's intent to stick to objectivity, state the bare facts, statistics, projections and consequential impacts of 'Contemporary Trends'; and refrain from making the categorical judgment calls on issues treated in the construction of the treatise so as not to stoke extant controversies or enflame new ones. Still, some readers may descry author's personal convictions, perspectives; moral, social, cultural values, and priorities.

Contemporary Trends

QUO Vadis: Whither are you going?

Drugs, Sex, Lifestyles, Conflicts: Abstract Studies and Reports; Projections, Predictions

CHARNJIT SINGH BAL

CONTENTS

PROLOGUE

DRUGS

LSD, Lysergsäure Acid Diäthylamid

Drug Decriminalization, Legalization

SEX

Sexual Gender, Diversity

Sexual Orientation

Sexual Preferences

Homosexuality

Controversy: Proponents, Opponents

Vigilante Rape,

Gang Rape

Warfare Rape, Sex Slaves

Child Molestation

SOCIAL

Capricious Spousal Relationships, Derelict Children,

HUMAN POPULATION EXPLOSION

IMPACTS

Ecological, Environmental, Urban Sprawls Resources
Depletion, Pollution

CONFLICTS

Political

Ideological

EPILOGUE

PROLOGUE

QUO VADIS: whither are you (We) going is an ancient, biblical-era Latin, interrogative term, which questions, and/or cautions the man, rather mankind about its contemporaneous trends divergent to its ancestral sexual preferences, life-styles, socio-cultural traditions and rectitude. The author, a lay empiricist came across the term that registered on his sub-conscience quite a while ago. It remained lackadaisical until it the nudged the author to verbalize the unconventional contemporary trends, personal lifestyles, familial relationships, promiscuous sexual revolution, decadent drug-culture and Global conflicts.

We, the humble humans who lack wherewithal to address, influence or change the mankind's contemporary trends; drug culture, personal relationships, lifestyles and global conflicts can draw absolution and succour from the veracious Latin adage '**Chesara, Sara, Sara; what will be, will be**' and '**Murphy's law; 'anything that can go wrong will go wrong'**. Or we can trust and pray to the almighty God to grant each of us wisdom and guidance,

'**God grant me the Serenity to accept the things I cannot change: Courage to change the things I can; and the Wisdom to know the difference.' Author Unknown**

Change is Law of Nature

Proverbially, the 'nature is in constant state of flux' or 'change is law of nature' i.e. nature changes periodically, geologically, ecologically, geographically and environmentally.

All the components of the divine nature's ecosystem, microcosm, organism, animals, including mankind, birds, bees; inanimate matter, geography; landscapes and environment undergo change.

Ecological rapport, i.e. harmonious relationship between organism, animates (animals), vegetation and inanimate matter and, benign environment and clement atmosphere is vital for the perpetual healthy global ecosystem,

Evidently, of all the innumerable animate species on the globe, mankind is the dominant specie which sets contemporaneous trends and engages in practices and pursuits; that impact the global ecology, ecosystem and atmosphere sooner or later.

While the changes effectuated by nature are usually gradual, systematic and indiscriminate, the changes wrought by mankind are often radical, whimsical and haphazard.

The impacts of Contemporaneous Trends, tendencies, pursuits and practices of mankind, whether good, bad or ugly are belated; i.e. they manifest decades, months, years or a century or so later.

The societal elders and leaders are role-models and their personal attitudes, life-styles, familial and social relationships influence and mould moral standards, social behavior and life styles of the rank and file, especially the juveniles who have intrinsic tendencies to imitate their elders, leaders and siblings.

The juveniles growing up in a permissive society with narcotics use, sexual promiscuity, capricious spousal relationships and life styles, naturally imitate prevailing personal lifestyles, social attitudes and familial relationships.

While some naïve juveniles make wrong choices, others are easily seduced or beguiled into choosing wrong lifestyles or relationships. In countries and jurisdictions with universal human rights, constitutional rights and civil rights guarantees combined with the judicial clause, 'accused are innocent until proven guilty', it makes difficult, if not virtually impossible for the jurists to prosecute the seducers or beguilers.

CHAPTER 1
DRUGS

Psychedelic Drugs; LSD

The English dictionaries describe LSD (Lysergsäure Acid Diäthylamid Drug), an illicit drug that causes psychotic symptoms similar to those of schizophrenia in user. Variety of the highly addictive LSDs, commonly dubbed by medical profession as mind altering drugs or psychedelics, are known and traded by fancy names in the drug culture, including producers, dealers and users.

The mind altering drugs or psychedelics are not new; these have been around ever since the advent of mankind on the good earth. However, since the onset of hippy culture in the 1960s, the use/abuse of illicit psychedelics or hallucinogenic drugs has skyrocketed and spread across all aspects of mankind.

In Montana, USA a father has been charged on 27 February for putting marijuana pipe in his 2-year old son's mouth to soothe him. The felony/misdemeanor was discovered by boy's grandmother, who found the video on her daughter's (cell) phone. The boy's father and mother told authorities they had given the boy the marijuana pipe to smoke 5 times in the past to calm him down. The couple's another new born baby tested positive for marijuana.

In a city school in Sonora, California, USA, a student found two 8-year-old and one 9-year-old third-grade students smoking marijuana in the school bathroom and reported to the school authorities, who called police.

Due to the psychedelic drugs' critical to chronic mental and physical health maladies; stupor, psychosis, hallucinations, schizophrenia, depression; HIV, AIDS, etc. and the overall detrimental impact on the society as a whole, the authorities have tried to prohibit sale and use of drugs in their respective jurisdictions.

The phenomenal surge in use/abuse and prohibition of illicit psychedelic drugs turned drug trade into highly lucrative, clandestine enterprise. Naturally the criminal elements, Mafia and Gangs, who thrive in the dark alleys of the underworld, were drawn to the clandestine trade and come to play dominant role in the production and supply of illicit psychedelic drugs.

The crafty criminal elements and organized crime cartels manage to outsmart or stay one step ahead of the Governments and authorities' attempts to prohibit production, distribution and consumption of illicit drugs. Reportedly, the illicit drugs are grown or produced in residential homes, industrial complexes, patches hidden in crops and remote thickets; and are smuggled by human mules via tunnels, small autos, large tractor trailers, ships, submarines and Aeroplanes.

Immeasurable, Interminable Costs

Apart from social, legal and financial costs there are immeasurable and interminable emotional costs associated with psychedelic drugs. The excruciating anguish and grief of loving parents, siblings or friends due to a chronic addict's reckless lifestyle, slow or sudden death are immeasurable and interminable.

A while ago a thirteen-year old Vancouver Island girl died of psychedelic drug abuse. Her two girl friends were lucky to escape tragic consequences. Since then many more LSD drug addicts have died lingering deaths or sudden deaths due to overdose, devastating the loving survivors.

Often the chronic drug addicts are rendered jobless, homeless, and driven to panhandle on' busy city street intersections and/or languish on the skid rows. Apparently, their life, for the most part, is fraught with utter privation and misery, except when they high on drugs that numb their mental faculty and induce fleeting euphoria. All LSD intoxications wane and the withdrawal induced depression and acute craving for drug, posses the addicts, who must procure drug at any cost, beg borrow or steal.

For the female addicts, drug procurement alternatives are often fraught with dire risks. Reportedly many end up as sex slaves in the hands of ruthless pimps, gangsters and organized crime syndicates. Some are bought and sold, kept captive and beaten to make them submissive. Many languish in the sex-slave trade. Very few ever escape or are rescued from the clutches of the vicious pimps and gangsters.

The unscrupulous drug pushers and ruthless sex trade agents, pimps come from all walks of life and demographic spectrum. Some drug dealers and pimps, reportedly start early in life, while they are still juveniles in the schools, where they start pushing drugs and recruiting naïve peers for prostitution. Instances of some parents deploying their own offspring into drug trade have been rumoured, even reported.

Decriminalization, Legalization of Drugs

Due to the proactive advocacy of the drug culture exponents, civil libertarians and rights' lobbies to decriminalize and legalize drugs, the authorities in many jurisdictions, especially the Western liberal democratic countries, have decriminalized and legalized production, sale and possession of drugs. With decriminalization and legalization of drugs the cash strapped Governments get to tap into revenue source instead of exorbitant expenditure on prohibition enforcement. The politicians, maybe, get to tap into drug culture vote bank.

Although proverbial jury on pros and cons of medical or recreational use of drugs is still out, many European and American nations and jurisdictions have already granted commercial licences to grow and sell marijuana for medical and recreational use. Many more are ready to jump on the band wagon and capitalize on the drug trade revenue source instead of exorbitant expense on drug prohibition enforcement.

Chronology of Pot Legalization in USA

On November 6th 2012 the State Authorities of Colorado and Washing States of USA got approval from the voters of their Legislative Assemblies constituencies to legalize production and sale of pot, marijuana. Some other States followed suit. So far twenty states in the United States of America have joined numerous jurisdictions that allow legal sale of marijuana.

California in 1996; Alaska, Oregon, Washington in 1998; Maine in 1999; Colorado, Hawaii, Nevada in 2000; Montana Vermont in 2004; Rhode Island in 2006; New Mexico in 2007; Michigan in 2008; Arizona, Washington D. C., New Jersey in 2010; Delaware in 2011; Connecticut, Massachusetts in 2012; New Hampshire and Illinois in 2013 have already fully or partly legalized, marijuana.

Alaska, Hawaii, Maine, Maryland, Montana Nevada, New York, Rhode Island and Vermont are considering part or full legalization of marijuana

An agent of North American NFL player suspended for repeated positive marijuana test results says, "If marijuana is legal in some *(US)* states I don't understand how an employer has the right to control what an employee does after working hours. It is just not right."

Buoyed by the US President, Barack Obama's call to the US Congress to soften penalties for the innocuous (less harmful) drugs, led the pot lobbyists, marijuana growers and retailers converged (March 2014) on the US Capital, Washington D. C. to persuade US Congress to expand marijuana legalization.

While many states and jurisdictions in the United States of America are jumping on the proverbial marijuana 'band wagon' and fast tracking marijuana decriminalization and legalization Netherland or Holland, the pioneer country to legalize recreational marijuana sale and smoking in country's coffee shops is backtracking its marijuana sale policy.

Having been unsuccessful earlier in an attempt to prevent the sale to the droves of cross border marijuana customers by introducing 'weed pass' for the Dutch citizens only, the Netherland government is reported to be taking hard line regarding sale of marijuana in the coffee shops especially in the border areas. The print media report does not specify definitive reasons for hard line measures.

Canadian Governments' Drug Laws Stymied

United States of America's next door neighbour, Canada's federal Government has enacted revised drug laws, part of Bill C-10 or Safe Streets and Communities Act effective April 1st 2014. But Canada may not be able to hold out much longer against marijuana industry, growers, sellers, users/abusers; and decriminalization and legalization lobby, politicians, academics, lawyers and jurists, journalists, et al critical of the act.

Essentially toughing the provisions to fight illicit production and sale of drugs and crime, the Canadian Federal Bill C-10 or Act drew criticism from protagonists of pot. A University of Victoria, BC Professor criticized the media for skewed reportage, politicians' reliance on misinformation and law enforcement agencies, especially RCMP for linking Marijuana production and distribution to gangs and other criminal syndicates.'

The Vancouver Sun Reporter, who posted script of his interview with the Professor wrote, "The RCMP, which the Professor focuses on in the book titled 'Killer Weed' declined to respond to her criticism."

Making a case for marijuana legalization, another Vancouver Sun columnist, wrote, "A 57 year-old habitual criminal and addict is the latest illustration of what is wrong with Ottawa's stiffen-the-rod approach to crime fighting."

"John Doe has been a nuisance in Victoria for most of his life – odd convictions for robbery, breaking and entering, and other property – related crimes."

"Yet despite his lengthy record of recidivism *(repetitive crime spree)*, the B.C. Court of Appeal recently refused a crown request to substantially increase his prison sentence for bank robbery."

"'This is a case involving no violence, except for an implied threat that accompanied the demand for money,' Justice....said."

".... is typical of the revolving-door offenders who commit a great portion of our crimes, cause most of the public disorder, and drive up policing and corrections costs because of their addictions and mental health problems."

"Like many addicts, he has not committed crimes of overt violence or weapons offences – he steals to feed a heroin habit that could be legally supplied for pennies."

A letter published in the paper's next issue wrote, "It is virtually impossible to find an addict of heroin, crack cocaine or crystal meth who is not a criminal. Addicts can easily have $100- to $200-daily habit. To support this requires multiple daily thefts from stores, cars, homes and people ... Substance Added public costs include police and hospital services."

The letter writer didn't suggest drug decriminalization or legalization, but wrote, "More than prison is required, for example, a controlled environment for criminal addicts, like remote work and skills development sites could be tried with treatment of addiction as the priority."

Another British Columbia Provincial Court Judge in Feb. 2014 ruled that Canadian Government's recently introduced minimum one-year mandatory sentence for drug trafficking is in violation of the charter of Rights.

'The judge sentenced the low-level drug dealer to 191 days imprisonment instead, citing that the dealer was selling drugs to feed his addiction. The 25-year old dealer who was convicted, in September 2011, of three counts for possession of crack (cocaine), methamphetamine and heroin for the purpose of pushing, reportedly, has had 21 previous convictions for forgery, larceny, illegal weapons possession and drug trafficking. With double credit for pretrial jail time he spent 27 days in jail. He committed 5 more offences while on bail.'

The scofflaws always find loophole, ways to skirt or stretch the prohibitive jurisdictional laws or bylaws to their advantage. One alleged case pertaining to licensed marijuana grow operations reported in print media reads 'an upscale Canadian suburban city (West Vancouver) Police raided a home where medical marijuana grow was authorized, and seized far more pot than permitted by Health Canada.

First responders were called to deal with reports of gas leak. Const .... .says officers entered the house after leak had been shut off and spotted more than 800 marijuana plants, with an estimated street value of about $244,000 at maturity.

The suburban city Police said the force was aware that the medical marijuana grow-op was allowed on the property, but noted it was restricted to no more than 161 plants. Along with the (800) plants, officers seized growing equipment and more than 1.7 kilograms of suspected marijuana bud, packaged in roughly quarter-kilogram bags. A criminal investigation is underway and police say it is too early to identify a suspect.'

A Canadian mega city (Vancouver) councillor and police say they won't be enforcing the Canadian federal government's law restricting licensed companies to produce and distribute medical marijuana. The councillor, who is not a medico, says that the federal law interferes with right of the people to access medicine. He reiterates, "It really is about access to medication, and the rules under new federal law would essentially bloc people from getting their medication. We just don't see these (unlicensed) medical marijuana dispensaries as something we need to shut down as long as they are only providing marijuana to people who medically need it"

The city police say they are aware of 29 illegal medical marijuana dispensaries in the city but they don't raid them as long as they sell to people who have medical marijuana permits. A police spokesman said, "We don't have plans for massive raids on April 2nd (2014)".

A lawyer representing a chronic addicts' group has petitioned a Vancouver judge to issue an injunction against Canadian Federal Health Minister's order to Health Canada staff to stop approving prescription drugs, heroin, cocaine and ecstasy. The Health Canada granted approval to procure prescription drugs to the addicts who had taken part in clinical trial study to test effectiveness of pharmaceutical-grade diacetylmorphine (heroin) and, hydromophone (methadone) at end of study.

The Minister said that Health Canada Staff granted approval through a loophole. "Heroin is a dangerous drug that destroys lives".

The lawyer told the judge 'Heroin addiction is a chronic disease which left untreated can be fatal. Depriving these chronic addicts of effective treatment is violation of their charter rights.'

A 'compassion club' pot grow owner-operator busted in 2011 and facing drug trafficking charge, is set to launch a lawsuit in a Canadian law court. The plaintiff says his lawsuit is a constitutional challenge to the Canadian Federal law banning such non-profit clubs from selling medicinal marijuana without licence, violates patients' charter rights.

Despite Federal Canadian laws restricting use of marijuana for medicinal purposes only, the scofflaws openly indulge in pleasure use of marijuana with virtual immunity, thanks to local authorities' condonation or apathy.

In Canada's mega city, Vancouver half a dozen men, reportedly, sit daily on the side walk in front of a bistro located on a typical family neighborhood street, smoking marijuana for pleasure and making passes at the female passersby.

The bistro owner claims smokers support local business and keep hardcore junkies and drug dealers from the neighborhood, to justify flouting the law.

Note:-The names in the above passages have been excluded.

With the numerous governments and jurisdictions jumping the band wagon to decriminalize and legalize marijuana production and distribution, the experts are predicting it to be the industry of the future, The proliferation of marijuana production, distribution and medicinal and recreational consumption gets all the more ominous with investment brokers and promoters soliciting for investment funds for the marijuana grow operations corporations.

In March 2014 'Tweed Inc.' became the first publically traded medical medicinal pot company in Canada.

The commercial marijuana grow operations will encroach upon agricultural lands, parks or forests already being lost to residential, industrial and infrastructure developments.

And the indoor marijuana grow operations are evidently source of nuisance and fire hazard in the residential neighbourhoods.

'An old mushroom barn modified for a 'licensed medicinal marijuana-grow operation' in Metro-Vancouver's suburb, Surrey went up in flames. Luckily many of the close proximity neighbours had moved away due to marijuana odour and 'scrubby people' loafing around. According to a resident neighbor "There were a lot of weirdoes around there."' Print media report

'According to 2010 RCMP report, 'medicinal marijuana grow operations fires across Canada were 24 times more likely in the *(indoor)* pot grow operations. In BC alone there were 36 fires in the last 8 years *(2006-14)*.

Arguably, extremely high fire hazard, high crime rate, health risks and over all damage control cost associated with marijuana production and consumption by far outweigh its benefits. The decriminalization and legalization of marijuana is unlikely to lessen the risks and costs.

When the Colorado voters approved legal sale of marijuana for recreational use they also voted 12.9 percent state tax and 15 percent excise tax on it. With the local jurisdictions tax an ounce of recreational can cost up to $400.00 US.

The black market drug pushers with no overhead costs, taxes or licences fees can sell the same quantity much cheaply. But evidently, black market drug trade too, has its dangers, prosecutions for possession of over legal limit,(one ounce marijuana); and ruthless underworld culture thuggery, rivalries, summary justice, etc.

Medical Marijuana Pushers

'Representatives for medical marijuana companies are sent to doctors' offices as part of push to get hesitant physicians to prescribe the drug more often.'

'It's a development that has dismayed Dr. Louis Hugo Francescutti, the president of the Canadian Medical Association, who says that largely unproven treatment is now being thrust upon doctors, putting them into potential confrontation with patients looking to score *(secure)* drugs and venders looking to peddle them.' "I am actually quite frightened." He said.

'Francescutti said some of Canada's 13 licensed marijuana producers are operating in the same way that pharmaceutical companies do.'

"They've got product they have to move. So they've hired the best advertising firms," he said. Now, they've got very professional, well dressed men and women knocking on doctors' offices." Print media report, July 24 2014

'These people have an agenda, they want to sell it, want to make money.' Ibid, **Dr. Alykhan Abdulla,** President, Academy of Medicine, Ottawa

Pot goes into **Slot**

A medical pot dispensing enterprise, "Pain society' has put pot into slots of a recently installed vending machine in its facility located in East Vancouver, B.C. The clients with doctor's note can buy hygienically packaged half-ounce bags of wide range of strains of pot at a price ranging from $12.00 to $50.00 Canadian.

The Society's ambitious director, Chuck Varabioff said that clients have embraced the new concept; and he envisions a day when he can install and service similar vending machines in every nursing home and medical clinic in Vancouver, with those facilities getting percentage of sales.

He said, "I won't do anything outside the city of Vancouver, which has a pretty liberal attitude about this *(pot)*, he said, "Eventually, I see this going Canada wide."

All drugs whether legal, illegal, medicinal or recreational are addictive and cause adverse side effects. The tobacco is known to be carcinogen, the marijuana could be worse.

"People think a little recreational marijuana use shouldn't cause problem. -. Our data directly says this is not so." Dr. Hans Breiter, professor of psychology, Northwestern University, BC

'Harvard Medical School researchers, reportedly, carried out detailed 3D scans of students who used cannabis.... Two major sections of the brain were found to be affected. They found that the more cannabis the students used, greater the (brain) abnormalities.'

"Drugs of abuse can cause more dopamine release than natural rewards like food, sex and social interaction. That is why drugs take on so much salience (importance), and everything else loses its importance. **Jodi Gilman**, researcher Massachusetts General Center, Addiction Medicine

The study is published in the journal of Neurosciences.

"For too long cannabis has been seen as a safe drug but, as this study suggests, it can have serious impact on your mental health. Research also shows that when people smoke cannabis before the age of 45, it quadruples their chance of developing psychosis. But very few are aware of the risks involved." **Mark Winsstanley**, Chief Executive, Mental Illnesses

Legal or not the drug use or abuse is on the on the rise and spreading across the globe rapidly.

The Chinese Government has issued a statute to test all 170 million kindergarten children for drugs. The discovery of kindergarten teachers secretly feeding the proscription drugs to prevent the pupils falling sick and optimize attendance prompted the ordinance. The kindergarten centers in china are paid for the day the pupil attends.

The Marijuana consumption apart from being health hazardous, its cultivation inside the houses, barns and buildings is source of high fire hazard and cause of structural damage

By all accounts drug culture, legal, illegal, good or bad, is spreading fast in significant segments of communities all over the globe. Although the drugs and paraphernalia producers, suppliers, users, abusers and libertarians in the western world have managed to get marijuana legalized and safe drug injection sites (in-sites) opened, arguments for and against (benefits or harm of) drug use/abuse persist.

Chapter 2
LIFESTYLE TRENDS

Spousal Relationships

Evidently the contemporary marriages do not last as long as they used to in the past. The Christian wedding vows, 'in sickness or health', 'rich or poor', 'till death do us apart' are not enduring. Similarly the vows or pledges taken at the weddings of almost all other religious communities don't last much longer either.

Many spousal couples split for myriad (numerous) reasons, caprice, jealousy, infidelity, incompatibility, social or financial opportunity; and remarry sooner or later. Some remarry several times, leaving behind trail of several, spouses, ex-wives or ex-husbands.

Then there are common-law relationship spouses who go through any number of common-law partners, girl-friends or boy-friends.

Derelict Children

Special bond between animal species' including mankind's biological parents and their offspring is a natural phenomenon Whenever the human biological parents split whether out of traditional heterosexual marriages, unions or common-law relationships, their children are usually left in a limbo. While some hapless children suffer psychological trauma, many others suffer mental distress, physical and/or sexual abuse in the orphanages, step or foster parents' homes.

The nagging sense of dereliction, insecurity, psychological trauma, physical and/or sexual abuse turn some of them into drug addicts, recluses, recalcitrant juvenile delinquents and/or felons,

Gender Diversity

There are variety of popularly known sexual gender anatomies and traits, male, female, asexual, hermaphrodite (dual male, female genitalia) eunuchs (castrated men-servants in harems, palaces) and androgynous, (dual sexual traits) in the animal species, particularly in mankind.

In the mankind there is another known category, the transgender, people born with sexual anatomies incompatible with their inherent sexual traits. They can have their genitalia changed surgically when they reach adulthood. Many do. Some demand and insist on gender change to suit their intrinsic sexual trait.

'Michelle Klosilek a transgender has received hormone treatments and lives as a woman in an all-male prison. Klosilek was named Robert when convicted of killing his wife in 1990. A federal judge ruled in 2012 'surgery is the "only adequate treatment" for Klosilek's gender identity disorder'. Prison officials appealed the ruling. Klosilek sued the Massachusetts department of justice after prison officials refused to grant her request for sex reassignment surgery. A US federal appeals court has upheld a judge's ruling granting a taxpayer-funded sex change for a transgender prisoner. The court ruled Friday the 64-year old Klosilek is entitled to the surgery'. Media report

Sexual Preferences

Apparently the omniscient God created two distinct genders, male and female, with congruent heterosexual sexual organs and anatomy conducive to reproductive function.

Our sage ancestors founded the chaste heterosexual self-sufficient family units and societal institutions based upon natural male and female anatomical endowments. They assigned them two distinct gender roles, father and mother, essential for familial functionality and human specie sustainability. To the male who is inherently endowed with physical prowess, they assigned the role of provider and protector. And to the female, who by nature is gentle, passive, patient and caring, they assigned the role of the nurturer and home maker.

The founders of world's half-dozen major religions integrated the divinity endowed heterosexual, male and female gender attributes essential for sustainable familial and societal disciplines into their respective religious creeds and traditions.

In non-human animal species, domestic or wild coitus is usually heterosexual and performed merely for procreation, periodically. But in the mankind coitus or copulation is performed for gratification, procreation, carnal lust and/or domination. See 'Holy Terror Unholy Tyranny', p 4

Mankind's sexual preferences categories include heterosexuality, homosexuality, bisexuality, lesbianism, sodomy and masochism. These sexual preference categories have been around ever since the advent of the mankind. But, the ancient murals, frescoes, artifacts, sculptures, socio-religious traditions, et al testify that the preference for heterosexuality has been foremost in the animal world including mankind since the prehistoric times. In all probability the heterosexuality lent itself instinctively to animal world due to animal species' male and female sexual organ congruency and functional procreation anatomy.

According to archeologists, anthropologists, evolutionists and paleontologists the humanoids evolved from and/or are genetically related to the primates, Gorillas, apes, monkeys, chimpanzees, et al. And recorded history, traditions and contemporary popular human coital preference testify that mankind is inherently heterosexual specie. However consistent with the maxim 'exception to the rule/norm', there have always been fringe human elements, Lesbians, Gays, Bisexuals, Trans-genders and Queers (LGBTQs) around.

Homosexuality

In the past homosexuality was kept secret for it was a taboo, stigma and crime. Since the 1960s hippie spawned sexual revolution the homosexuals have been coming out of the proverbial closet all over the globe. They come from all walks of life, prominent males, females, professionals, leaders and rank and file.

The homosexual communities are minorities still, but are proliferating globally, especially in the West, where homosexuality is celebrated on the main streets of metropolises featuring carnival-like parades with bedecked floats; and lesbians, gays, bisexuals, trans-genders and queers (LGBTQs) attired in scanty, gaudy and flamboyant apparels frolicking and flaunting homosexuality-culture, solidarity and gay pride.

Homosexuality, Bisexuality Abet STDs

'The Public Health officials in B.C. *(Canada)* are calling on sexually active gay and bisexual men to regularly get tested for syphilis after the number of new infections in the province doubled in 2012.' Print Media Report, June 2013

"Men who have sex with men are very much at increased risk right now and need to be tested every three to six months." Dr. Reka Gustafson, Medical Health Officer, Vancouver Coastal Health, B.C.

'About 80 percent of new cases have occurred among men who have sex with men…'

"Syphilis can appear to be very minor infection in its early stages. Some people don't have any symptoms at all. Others develop a chancre (open sore) that's completely painless. Chancres are found around the genitals, the anus and mouth but can be found wherever the bacterium entered the body." Ibid

'If the bacterium, Treponema pallidum isn't caught in early stages, it becomes latent in a person's body. When it becomes active again it can cause brain damage, strokes, blindness and even death.'

'The overall rate of new HIV *(Human Immune-deficiency Virus)* infection has steadily declined in British Columbia, but the epidemic among gay and bisexual men continues....

'Gay and bisexual men continue to bear a disproportionate burden of HIV illness.' Dr. Perry Kendall, Provincial Health Officer, Print media report, July 15 2014

Homosexuality: Societal Perspective

Since time immemorial the institution of traditional family-unit, i.e. biological father, mother and their biological children, has prevailed as a viable model.

Although the world wars, industrial, socio-cultural and sexual revolutions have rendered some of the gender roles reversible but the essential gender roles and features, sexual organ congruity, reproductive anatomy and nurturing functions remain immutable.

The homosexual familial unions can provide some of the basic necessities of family life but it is the heterosexual family-unit that is adequately equipped to provide all the familial requisites, biological parenthood, intuitive suckling, bonding, nurture, love, sense of security and belonging.

The sexual revolution, thanks to hippies, has gradually changed the very attitude of global societies regarding homosexuality from condemnation to condonation.

Just as legalization and decriminalization of drugs case, the Western Nations, European and American countries have taken lead to legitimize homosexual spousal Unions; and grant benefits and rights to the homosexual couples and dependents, same as the traditional heterosexual spousal families only.

Monkey see monkey do

The children learn instinctively by copying their parents, older siblings, peers and societal role models. Naturally homosexual or heterosexual environment is a significant factor in influencing a child's conception of normal sexuality.

Homosexuality Proponents vs. Opponents

The contemporary homosexuality trend has split communities, especially in the western hemisphere, into two camps, 1) Recently liberated homosexual exponents, civil libertarians, Charter and human rights advocates 2) Old guard traditionalists, moralists, ethicists and religionists.

In California, USA a high-tech gadget, Internet Browser Mozilla Firefox CEO, who had donated $1000.00 US in 2008 campaign to support proposed amendment banning same sex marriages in California, was fired.

The same sex marriage Mozilla employees and users had protested the donation earlier. But the protest escalated when the donor was promoted to the CEO position.

Homosexuality: International Diversity

The proliferating homosexuality trend has evoked diverse attitudes towards contemporary socio-cultural phenomenon in global communities and nations.

While homosexuality is legal in the European and American countries it is disdained, denounced, prohibited and condemned in the Islamic Arabian and African countries; and tacitly condoned in the secular Asian countries.

Recently the Western bloc's fervid pro-homosexuality lobby and media criticised Russia's intent and efforts to curtail homosexuality propaganda during the 2014 Winter Olympics. While some homosexual athletes threatened to boycott the games, a Canadian mega city councillor travelled to 2014 Winter Olympic venue Sochi, Russia to participate in the fledgling Russian homosexual community's protest.

Reportedly, even before the 2014 Winter Olympics at Sochi, Russia, the Russian homosexuals had been seeking refuge in Canada, where homosexuality is legal. A Canadian immigration lawyer who specializes in Russian refugee claims of LGBTQs said that he normally handled couple of dozen such cases a year from Russia; but after the enactment of Russian anti-gay laws, the number of Russian gays seeking asylum in Canada has increased significantly.

Although Hong Kong, a virtual autonomous territory of china, decriminalized homosexuality in 1991, it doesn't sanction homosexual unions. In 2012 Hong Kong's tycoon father offered 500 million Hong Kong Dollars ($71.8 million Cdn) to any potential male suitor who would woo his lesbian daughter who had eloped with her partner to France, where Christian Church blesses homosexual marriages.

Uganda Defies Western Nations

"'KAMPALA, Uganda – Uganda is willing to give up all international aid to keep its new anti-homosexuality law and "save gays from damnation" its ethics Minister said as the World Bank followed other donors and froze $100 million US new loan.'

Vatican Cardinal Blasts Anti-Gay Law

'A Vatican cardinal has criticized Uganda's anti-gay law and called for the repeal of its severe penalties. Cardinal Peter Turkson of Ghana, president of the 'Pontical Council for Justice and peace said Tuesday that "homosexuals are not criminals" and shouldn't be sentenced to life in prison. Speaking to reporters in Bratislava during a human rights conference, Turkson said the Vatican also calls on international community to keep providing aid.' Ibid

'Condemnation of new law by Western nations, which together give Uganda more than $1.67 billion a year aid drew quick criticism from Uganda's Ethics Minister, Simon Lokodo, who said, "We want to rid this country of homosexuality and if that means that people, Obama, Hague, you name them, want to stop their aid then let them. We don't need (aid), we won't die poor, and we will at least be able to save these gays from damnation."

In March 2014, Uganda passed the new anti-homosexuality law. 'Judges can now jail for life people who have gay sex. Those who "aid or abet" homosexuality, or fail to report suspected homosexuals, face terms up to 14 years'.

Apparently, not all Ugandans condone Government's anti-homosexuality stance.

'Since the new anti-homosexuality law was passed on Monday, "dozens" of gay people had been threatened with violence, evicted from their homes, or lost their jobs.' Sandra Ntebi gay activist

'Kelly Mukwano, 24 told *the* Daily Telegraph that his landlord evicted him this week after two years just because he was gay. "He said people knew I was homosexual, and he could not guarantee my safety. They could come and kill me any time. When I left people were staring, whispering. I did not realize the danger I was in."

'Akram described how his mother and sister threw him out of his family home after his name and photograph appeared in a tabloid story "outing" people as gay.'

Homosexuality: Religious Stance

Proverbially 'Man reaps what he sows'. Same can be said for a societies and civilizations.

In religious context the proverb alludes to divine judgement, i.e. restitution for compliance or retribution for noncompliance of various religions' doctrines. Arguably, that is why scriptures of all the major religions of the world don't condone open homosexuality, let alone sanction it. Islam entices male Jihadists to martyrdom with sex with young boys in paradise only, not on earth.

Dictionaries define Sodomy unnatural homosexual act, and impute it to **Sodom**, an ancient city around Dead Sea. It, and its sister city, Gomorrah, are said to have been destroyed by God for the wickedness of their inhabitants. See Bible, Old Testament, Genesis XVIII-XIX (18. 19)

Jesus Christ, before whose advent God is said to destroyed cities of Sodom and Gomorrah, warns mankind,

"On judgment day God would be more sever with cities rejecting the *(Biblical)* Gospel than he had been with Sodom and Gomorrah" Jesus Christ (Matt. 10:15, 11:22-24)

Homosexual Lobby Vs Christian University

The homosexual marriages have been legal in Canada since 2005, but the private Christian Trinity Western University requires all its students to sign a covenant that forbids them from engaging in sexual activity except in heterosexual marriages; and requires them to report violation of covenant.

The covenant opponents, Trial Lawyers Association of B.C. Lawyers' Rights Watch, legal Leaders for Diversity, National Association of Women, Center for feminist Legal Studies, student societies of law schools and law faculties of UBC (University of BC) and UVIC (Victoria); and the TWU covenant supporters, Catholic, Baptist, Mormon and Seventh-day Adventist Churches and (surprisingly) B.C. Civil Liberties Association made submissions to BC Law Society to rule on accreditation of Law School at Trinity Western University in light of its covenant.

The BC Law society ruled in University's favor; and Advance Education Minister approbated (approved) the Law Society's ruling. But the contentious issue is far from over. A young Vancouver Parks board Commissioner Trevor Loke, an openly gay Christian alleges Minister's approbation is discriminatory and has petitioned BC Supreme Court to overturn the Minister's approbation.

Christian Family Quits Boy Scouts

A 15-year-old kid, just months away from becoming coveted 'Eagle Scout', has quit mixed sexuality 'Boy Scouts of America'. His family's men, including his older brother had been 'Eagle Scouts' for four generations.

It was a difficult decision for the Christian family as the boy had aspired and toiled for years to achieve 'Eagle Scout' and higher ranking in the century-old 'Boy Scouts of America' that had started to recruit homosexual boys recently.

The boy's devout Christian father said "homosexuality is a sin that cannot be tolerated. As Christians from a scriptural basis, we love all folks, but the scripture is very clear that being homosexual is a sin. We have got to be able to hold a strong line and set a consistent example for our young men".

Both, the father and son have left the 'Boy Scouts of America' and along with some other like-minded Christian families have set up another parallel organization, 'Trail Life' based on Christian values. The organizers of 'Trail Life' say 'they are fighting for the traditional values of Christianity and scouting, including the scout oath "morally straight" – in the face of America's growing acceptance of gays and gay marriages.

The 'Trail Life' organizers reportedly left the 'Boy Scouts of America' because 'the scouting ideals they knew have changed. They say 'the *(new)* organization welcomes all boys who don't engage or promote sexual immorality. So far boys, mostly from Boy Scouts, have joined 'Trail Life' that has grown to 600 units in more than 40 states'.

A small Church Pastor, who preached for couple of decade in a USA town, said, "The US is doomed because of its tolerance of homosexuality" (Sic). The homosexuality proponents branded him 'Homophobic Pastor'.

Sikhism espouses Heterosexuality Only

Sikhism is an acclaimed ecumenical religion for its inclusive creed co-authored by savant Sikh Gurus; and 15 multi-faith and multi-caste holy sages. Discerning divine schema of vital human specie's procreation function and essential sexual gratification need, Sikh scriptural anthology co-authors professed lasting, chaste, monogamous, heterosexual marriage/s only.

"They (Sikh scriptures).are compact in spite of length and are a revelation of the human heart, varying from the most noble *(monotheistic)* concept of God, to the recognition and indeed insistence upon the practical needs of human body." **Pearl S. Buck, Noble Laureate**

The centrality of Sikh theology is 'spiritual reunion of immortal, asexual spirit with its divine source or origin, i.e. primal spirit variously called Great Spirit, Jehovah, God, Allah or Bhagwan, et al.

The Sikh Canon draws analogy between mundane marriage of a man and woman; and; spiritual union of the metaphoric soul-bride and divine husband, God. The verses of the Sikh wedding ceremony's hymn articulate the analogy.

"Having discerned all *(mundane)* relations, (attachments) are transitory; I tie knot (attach myself) to you (God)". G.G. P. 963

Corporeally the hymn's verses express mundane female bride's wedding vow, "Having found my nativity relations temporary, I conjugate with you (bridegroom)".

Spiritually the hymn's verses connote metaphoric soul-bride's spiritual union with its divine master (husband).

Essentially the hymn's verses depict transition of a single woman to a happily married woman; or transition of a materialistic person to a devout, pious and righteous person.

Sikh apocrypha legends, tales and traditions too narrate heterosexual marriages, relationships and liaisons only.

Islam condemns Homosexuality

Islam doctrinally and traditionally condemns homosexuality. In many Islamic Nations homosexuality is a crime, punishable up to life in jail, even death.

'Indeed, you approach man with *(sexual)* desire, instead of woman rather, you are a transgressing people.' Holy Qur'an, Surah 7, 81

'And Allah made for you spouses from among yourselves, and produced for you from spouses children and grandchildren,' Ibid, Surah 16, 72

'The traditional schools of Islamic law, based on Qur'anic verses and Hadith, consider homosexual act a punishable crime and a sin, and influenced by Imam Malik and Imam' Shafi in Islam.' Wikipedia

'Today in most of the Islamic world homosexuality is not socially or legally accepted. In nine Muslim countries, Afghanistan, Iran, Mauritania, Nigeria, Saudi Arabia, Somalia, Sudan, the UAE, and Yemen, homosexual activity carries the death penalty.' Ibid

In early 2014, the Nigerian President, Goodluck Jonathan signed the 'Same-sex prohibition act'. Dubbed as 'Jail the gays' bill, it criminalizes homosexual institutions; gay marriages and organizations. Associated Press report

'Soon after Same-sex prohibition enactment, Nigeria's Bauchi state police arrested 11 gay men accused of belonging to gay organization.' "11 gay men have been arrested in the past two weeks." Mustapha Baba, Chairman, Bauchi State Sharia Commission Ibid

"The witch hunt all began in Bauchi State with a wild rumour that they *(US)* had paid gay activists $20 million to promote same-sex marriages in this highly religious and conservative nation." **Dorothy Aken'Ova**

AIDS Counsellor, International Center for Reproduction and Sexual Right, Nigeria Ibid

'Bauchi has Sharia, Islamic Law enforced in nine of thirty six States of Nigeria and Western-style *(secular)* penal code.'

'Thousands of protestors threw stones into a Sharia court Wednesday, urging the speedy convictions and executions of 11 men arrested for belonging to gay organizations. Security officials fired into the air to disperse protestors in Bauchi, a city in northern Nigeria so the accused men could be safely returned to the prison. The Judge El-Yakubu Aliyu abruptly closed the court." (Sic) Print Media Report

Gay sex acts would be punishable in Indonesia

'People caught having homosexual sex could be publically caned in Indonesia's conservative Aceh province if an Islam-inspired draft law is approved..... Lawmaker Mohamrriad Syafari said a majority of provincial lawmakers supported criminalizing gay sex... Ibid

Homosexuality Curable

'Spain's newly appointed cardinal insisted that homo-sexuality can be cured with treatment and linked it to other "bodily deficiencies" such as high blood pressure.' Fernando Sebastian'

'Cardinal) Aguilar, 84 said, "Homosexuality is a deficient way of manifesting sexuality because (sexuality has a structure and a purpose, which is procreation".

Currently many 'Governments in Western World are granting equal rights and benefits to homosexuals and homosexual families in par with the traditional heterosexual family units. And as the rest of the nationalities copy the western world's socio-cultural mores and lifestyles, its contemporary homosexuality trend and homosexual family unions are, inevitably, going to spread across the cross section of the global community at large, sooner or later.

Chapter 3

PERVERSE SEXUAL TRENDS

Due, perhaps, to the modern advanced and fast communications modes incidents of heinous rape are reported worldwide in print and on broadcast media much more frequently. The flurry of child molestations, rape, vigilante and gang rapes reports coming out of India and its capital, New Delhi, testify to these being notorious country and city for sexual assaults.

Vigilante Rape

'An authoritarian tribal village elder, in rural area of West Bengal state, India ordered gang rape of a Hindu tribal girl for allegedly having love affair with a married Muslim man.

A Santhal tribe's 20 year old girl reported to the local police that because her family couldn't pay the fine for the alleged affair, she was untied from a tree in the village, Subalpur, taken to a thatched shed and gang raped for six hours by thirteen men of victim's village. Included in fiendish gang was the deviant village elder who had ordered the vigilante rape. One of the 300 witnesses of kangaroo court trial recorded the proceedings on Cellular/mobile phone. Reportedly, the Birbhum district's local Police have in their possession the gang rape footage too, also captured on cellular/mobile phone.

Another media report of the same diabolical gang rape episode states that the village council ruled that the accused girl pay fifty thousand Rupees – approximately $800.00 Canadian, which the poor aboriginal girl's family couldn't pay for it subsists on $2.00 or less per day, On village council head's order 13 perverts, including the council head, gang-raped the girl throughout the night of January 20, 2014.

The family reported the abhorrent act to the Labhpur police station in Birbhum district of West Bengal, India.

This vigilante rape case is by no means isolated. Similar vigilante gang rape cases of women in rural India and Pakistan have also been reported in media, recently.

Similarity of Indian and Pakistan's rural/tribal draconian justice systems is not surprising since the Indian Sub-Continent's multi socio-religious and cultural community at large has lived together for centuries until recently. Indian Sub-Continent was partitioned into India and Pakistan in 1947. There is still a large Muslim minority living India, just as there is a small Hindu minority living in Pakistan.

The rural Indian sub-continent's village councils adjudicate wide range of cases, including moral, socio-cultural issues, dress codes, property disputes, et al. The elders of Indian sub-Continent's tribal communities are law into themselves.

In the tribal communities the council elders' wield much more authority than the state enforcement authorities. Even the police concede that the tribal people do not obey the state statutes as readily as the rest of the people. They fear their council elders more than the state law enforcement agencies.

The Supreme Court of India, noting that the cult and caste prejudiced tribal justice system hampers the advancement of the tribal communities in literacy and economic fields, ordered the state Governments in 2011 to restrain the authoritarian tribal council elders who enforce the draconian prejudicial justice system.

The Supreme Court of India's order has remained unheeded so far. The tribal peoples, especially women who defy arbitrary tribal law, still, face being ostracised, beaten or killed to restore family, clan or tribal honor.

Gang Rape

The brutal gang rape of a 23-year old physiotherapist student, Joyti Singh in Delhi is epitome of horrid gang rape. To call the evil predators, animals, is insult to the animals.

No normal human being, listening or reading the account of the heinous act, can escape the heart wrenching impact of the horrific imagery of the excruciating ordeal the poor girl must have suffered.

The dying statement of Joyti Singh details the evil deed of the devil-incarnate gang rape culprits. The statement recorded on video tape, states that Joyti Singh and her student friend, Awninder Panday left Delhi's cinema hall and boarded a bus with six men including the driver and conductor in it. The student pair, despite the ominous intuition paid the fares sat down for the bus ride.

The six men, including a juvenile turned out to be fiendish thugs. The conductor closed doors, turned off the lights, approached the student couple and initiated the assault. Without provocation he started beating the male student. The other thugs joined the assault. They held the male, Awninder and took Joyti to back of the bus, tore her clothing and took turns, raping her and driving the bus. They, not only raped her for an hour, but also bit her all over her body and beat her with iron rod.

The student couple's fierce fight and frantic screams were of no avail. The despicable thugs took all their belongings and cell phone, stripped both students naked and threw the victims out of the moving bus. The folks who found them lying naked on side of the road notified the police.

Joyti Singh succumbed to, savage gang rape ordeal, vicious beatings and internal injuries caused by atrocious assault, two weeks later in a Singapore hospital, where doctors had to remove ninety five percent of her ruptured innards.

It is feared the Juvenile perverted fiend, who reportedly committed horrid atrocities causing internal injuries with a steel rod, might escape full judicial retribution. It would be travesty of justice, if he did.

Gang Raped Victim Faces Lashes

Reportedly, 8 men burst into a 25 year old **Indonesian Muslim** widow's home, found her with a married man. They beat the man, and gang raped the woman and then handed the couple to the Islamic police for having consensual sex.

Reportedly, the district head of Islamic law, Sharia is reported to have recommended that the couple be administered 9 lashes, for violating Islamic law, Sharia, i.e. 'being in the same room together and getting ready to engage in consensual sex, or admission of having had consensual sex earlier.

It is inconceivable that Sharia, Islamic jurisprudence would sanction rape. If it does, it is travesty of justice.

Rape, Gang Rape Pandemic

"Last year (2012) almost 65,000 sexual offences were reported to South African police, which estimates a woman is raped there every 36 seconds." Craig & Marc KIELBURGER

India, where a woman is, reportedly raped every 22 minutes, lies in third place, after 2nd place Brazil, in the rape or gang rape pandemic.

Warfare Rape, Sex Slaves

The rape and sex slavery of hapless enemy women during warfare have happened ever since the advent of mankind on the face of the earth.

Recently the Japanese government apologised for the enslavement and sexual exploitation of Asian women during its invasion of neighboring countries. Japanese soldiers enslaved about 200,000 Asian women, for their pleasure.

The sex slavery of Asian women by the Japanese invaders is not an isolated instance. The recorded history and traditions witness to sex slavery by soldiery of almost every nation, race, ethnic or religious community.

Evidently, India's Capital city Delhi is world's gang rape capital; and India and Pakistan are hot-beds of vigilante rape, gang rape and child molestation; the African Nations are the hot-beds of warfare rape where alleged enemy women are raped by the militias. The democratic Republic of Congo is probably world's worst warfare rape zone.

'It is estimated more than 200,000 women have been raped in the civil war since 1998. In the northeast of the country (Republic of Congo), a criminal militia is now waging war to control rich local minerals, timber and wildlife resources. This militia is alleged to have abducted some 3,000 women to use as sex slaves." Craig & Marc KIELBURGER

Child Molestation

Child molestation is another heinous crime perpetrated by contemptible predatory men all over the world. But the flurry of Media reports of the child molestation in New Delhi by the detestable men; neighbors, relatives and/or family friends, makes India's capital city world's child molestation capital too.

Very few sexual assaults are ever reported due to the intimidation, shame and stigma attached to the heinous crime. The Muslim women are required to produce four eye witnesses to the rape if they want to get justice from the male-dominated Islamic jurists.

The only deterrent to the widespread heinous vigilante rape, gang rape and child molestation trend may be to emasculate or castrate the sexual predators. It is a draconian measure, but it is the only deterrent we can think of to safeguard the hapless sexual preys.

Honor Killing

Honor killings are mostly committed in the theocratic and semi-theocratic Islamic nations; and in secular nations with Islamic socio-cultural population mix and influence for instance multi-cultural India that was ruled by Muslim Mogul dynasty for two medieval centuries.

With the contemporary global migration trend the migrants bring with them their native countries' socio-cultural traditions and customs to the new countries of domicile.

Recently an Afghan family which migrated to Canada killed their three young daughters who tried to emulate their Canadian peers. The girls' father, mother and brother were convicted of drowning homicide of three girls and their stepmother.

In Gaza strip and Palestinian West Bank, situated in the Islamic heartland, twenty six women, twice the number in the previous year, were reportedly killed by the relatives in 2013 AD.

In September 2013 a Palestinian brother strangled his 21-year-old mentally disabled sister allegedly over family honor. In January/February 2014, another 21-year-old brother stabbed his 18-year-old sister, who was praying at time, to death, for the same reason.

An honor killing per se is culpable homicide. But not all honor killings are committed for the purported reasons.

"In some cases, perpetrators claimed to have killed in name of family honor when in fact they appeared to have had financial or other motives and hoped to benefit from relatively lenient punishments". **Rabiha Diab**, West Bank Women's Affairs Minister

The honor killings of 'women only', is indicative of highly biased, male-dominated socio-cultural customs, traditions and draconian justice. No man has ever suffered the same tragic fate as the women who are killed to restore family, clan or tribe's honor. Often women are killed on mere suspicion and perpetrators escape punishment. There is no indication, that honor killing of 'women only' will be crime of the past, anytime soon.

Acid Attacks

More recently women in the Indian Subcontinent, India, Pakistan and Bangladesh are plagued by another cowardly, horrendous crime; acid attacks that kill them, or worse disfigure beautiful women and force them to a life of mental anguish and isolation. The beautiful, exuberant girls are turned instantly into grotesque objects driven to sulking and seclusion.

In committing this hideous crime too, the despicable fiends on the Indian Subcontinent, lead rest of the world.

Acid attack is another hideous crime that deserves **'eye for an eye'** retribution.

The rape, sexual assaults, honor killings and acid attacks are heinous felonies that render the victims traumatized and anguished for rest of their life, but the perpetrators go scot-free or get slap on the wrist.

HUMAN POPULATION EXPLOSION

Historical demographics and Anthropological studies evidence that it took couple of millennium/s for the human population to grow to one billion in numbers. But it has taken less than a century and a half for the human population to grow to seven billion and surpass earth's optimal carrying capacity. It is growing rapidly and is projected to grow to fourteen billions by the mid 21st century.

As the human population increases, so does its encroachment upon the arable land and wilderness. Paradoxically, the human population increases at the cost of other animal species. But divine god or some other mystical supernatural power keeps the total number of the (predominant) mankind and other animal species constant.

The paradox supports Eastern religions' tenet that **all animals are endowed with souls**. Essentially, animal means 'a living body endowed with animation or mobility, as opposed to inanimate (immobile) matter. Arguably, Soul animates an animal, i.e. no soul, no animation. Departed soul leaves behind a dead body.

Dominant Mankind

Evidently the impact of the predominant mankind on the global ecosystem, including other animal species, landscape, resources and environment, is cataclysmic.

Compared to the non-human-animal species, mankind requires lot more space for habitat, infrastructure, utilities, transportation, industry, retail facilities, socio-cultural facilities, et al; and consumes lot more globe's limited resources, produces cataclysmic pollution, humongous garbage and/or waste; and devastates the good earth with invasive resource extraction operations, warfare explosives, et al.

Urban Sprawls, Concrete Jungles

As mentioned above, human population growth has surpassed good Earth's optimal carrying capacity. Due to the exponential Human population growth, the mega cities worldwide have grown to urban sprawls. The suburbs have lost rustic character and ground to urbanization and densification. Their good old landscapes featuring vestiges of tranquil greenery, open spaces has been replaced with concrete jungles; dotted with skyscrapers, strata complexes, multiplexes and monster houses.

Naturally, the urbanization increases hustle and bustle; and densification increases congestion, transmission of contagious and infectious diseases risks, noise pollution and strain neighbourly cordiality. The skyscrapers, strata complexes, multiplexes and monster houses jeopardize the privacy of the residents of the older smaller houses.

With the human population growth the older smaller cities have grown to sprawling metropolises and good old towns have lost their spacious, hinterland character to metropolitan urban hustle and bustle.

And the mushrooming urban sprawls and sprawling metropolises are putting squeeze, not only on the urban, suburban vestiges of serene greenery, open spaces, but also on hinterland arable lands, wilderness and wild animal habitats.

The wild animals deprived of habitats and sustenance, stray into the human habitats in search of forage and refuge. The human response is either to capture and relocate or kill the stray wild animals.

Dire Consequences, Predictions

Evidently, as the human population grows so do the pollution, garbage, contamination of arable land and water resources.

Simple logic dictates that more the human population, more the agricultural land required for growing more food. But with mankind's phenomenal population increase the agricultural land is being appropriated rapidly for human habitats and infrastructure use. The non-agrarian use and contamination of agricultural land; and cataclysmic weather; droughts, floods spell famines.

If the projection that the human population will double itself i.e. grow to 14 billion by 2050 AD materializes, mankind will be hard put to deal with the dire consequences, i.e. smothering pollution, acute shortages of food and fresh water resources. Recent scientific studies already predict that future wars will be waged over water.

The reports that many global communities are already suffering due to shortages of food and fresh water lend credulity to the looming wars over water resources.

The United States' prime agriculture and horticulture state, California that produces quarter of county's food supply is anticipating drastic reduction in its ability to grow crops, vegetables and fruits in the central valley in the future due to repeated droughts. Print Media Report

While the looming wars over water are awe inspiring, the predicted flooding of lowlands; habitats and arable lands due to melting polar ice and rising sea level caused by soaring global temperature, is all the more worrisome.

The Cryostat space craft, a radar instrument designed to calculate the height and shape of the polar ice sheet, launched by European Space Agency, has been studying changes at the poles since 2010. New data from Cryostat indicates increased melting in west Antarctic could raise sea level by 1.2 meters. Geophysical Research Papers

POLLUTION

The divinity created and equipped divine nature to provide the various components of creation with life sustaining supplies, resources, and necessary means and capacity to maintain and/or restore environment; and ecosystem to congenial state. However mankind's contemporary trends, pursuits, indulgences and egregious consumption of global resources have rendered the nature inadequate to process and recycle its domestic, biological, industrial and vehicular waste.

The pollution and garbage are correlated and spread worldwide, on land, in the air and water. The major sources of pollution and garbage are fossil fuel by-products, combustion emissions, industrial processes' tailings, agricultural fertilizers, plastics, cleaners, effluent, domestic waste, personal effects etc.

The stratosphere's ozone layer that protects life on earth from ultraviolet Rays has been punctured with massive holes that are growing at an alarming rate. The vital basic necessity, potable water is reported to have been polluted with effluent, toxins and carcinogens.

India's holiest river Ganga (Ganges) is reported to be heavily polluted with effluent, industrial waste, and cremation debris; partially cremated corpses, and ashes. Its sister holy river, Jamuna, has reportedly surpassed it in pollution.

Jamuna is worshipped along with Ganges as one of the Hinduism's two holiest rivers.' Print media report

'The growth in Delhi's population to 22 million and rise of illegal slums has led to great increase in human waste and rubbish, much of which is dumped in the river. More than 1.5 billion litres of sewage enters the river from

Delhi's drains each day without passing through city's treatment plants.' Ibid

'Human ashes, leather tanning chemicals, pesticides and religious painted idols all add to the toxicity.' Ibid

'The Jamuna's black, foaming water has been compared with the Thames during the great stink of 1858 and long been an embarrassment to the Indian government.' Ibid

Aerial pollution in **China** forced the Airports to shutdown, and vulnerable people to stay indoors and others to wear respiratory masks outdoors in 2013.

'A senior government official has announced that two per cent arable land in China can't' *(be)* used for crops, due to pollution.' Print Media Report

'More than three million hectares, 7.5 million acres of China's farmland are too polluted with heavy metal and other chemicals to use for growing food.' Cabinet official, Ibid

'Air pollution in china, the world's biggest carbon emitter, has reached intolerable levels and the country should aggressively cut its reliance on coal, according to the National Center for Climate Change Strategy and International Cooperation.'

There is a glimmer of optimism, as the devastating impact of pollution on the arable land; environment and people's health has prodded the Chinese government out of oblivion. Heeding the wakeup call the Chinese government has committed itself to tackle the catastrophic pollution.

'China's environment ministry said Sunday, (23 February 2014) it had sent inspectors to Beijing and other areas of the country to look at polluting industries and check construction sites amid spell of severe air pollution.' Print Media Report

'China has become the world's biggest investor in the global trillion-dollar renewable energy market, which has helped pull down the capital cost of producing renewable electricity to the point where it is competitive with existing sources.'

"Through the ramp up of manufacturing (of wind turbines and solar panels) in China, it has helped reduce the costs of clean energy for everybody." **Ethan Zindler**, Head Analyst for Americans at Bloomberg New Energy Finance

GARBAGE

Evidently the mankind has littered globe's land, seas, rivers and streams with garbage. The developed nations are hard put to find and manage garbage dump sites. The developing nations' authorities are either ill equipped, lack means or will to manage garbage. Peoples dump garbage anywhere and everywhere landscaping whole the countries with ugly garbage.

The oceans are littered with large Islands of floating plastic Debris. The non-degradable stringy plastics get wrapped around the sea creatures with fatal consequences. The ingestion of micro-plastic particles misleads the marine food chain organism to feel full and starve to death.

'Water samples taken from inshore to 1,200 Kilometers off B.C. Canada coast were found to be contaminated with typically the size of coffee ground, 200 to 279 particles per cubic meter. The situation could worsen as small plastic particles from the Japanese earthquake in 2011 continue to drift to B.C. waters.' Print media Report

'Samples taken by the Canadian Coast Guard ship John P. Tully in 2012 showed a mean *(plastic)* particle size of 606 micrometer. About 75 per cent of particles were fragments and fibre derived from the deterioration of larger products, perhaps from coloured textiles such as acrylics released during laundry.' Ibid

Evidently, as the human population grows so do contamination of land, water and air with pollution and garbage. It stands to logic, the animal species will all be chocking in smog and wallowing in garbage; and suffering from food and water shortages.

Despite the projections and predictions of multitudinous mankind, its leadership is, seemingly, oblivious to the crucial impacts on the global environment and ecosystem.

Instead of attempts to control human population growth, the politicians; employers and business communities and ethnic communities' leaders keep pushing for more population growth for short term gains. To the business communities, population growth means more consumers. To the politicians and ethnic community leaders, it means more political clout. To the employers and governments it means more workers competing for the low wage jobs.

Chapter 4

POLITICAL IDEOLOGICAL POWER BLOCS

In the aftermath of the Second World War, the countries on the good earth were divided two major financial and political ideological blocs, capitalist and communist. The US led North American and western European countries and their satellites allied into capitalist bloc. And Union of Socialist Soviet Republic, (Russia with its Eastern annexed European countries) China, North Korea, and Vietnam constituted communist bloc. The former, US led bloc was dubbed as Capitalist bloc or first World and the latter USSR led bloc was dubbed as Communist bloc or second World.

The political ideology of first world Nations is rooted in **Magna Carta,** 'the great charter of rights and liberties' promulgated on 19 June 1215 AD, by English **King John**, boasts of democratic political system, 'of the people, by the people, for the people' in which the supreme power is held in the hands of the people and is administered through the elected legislators and parliamentarians who constitute laws.

The political ideology of communist bloc or Second world is entrenched in Marxist, Leninist socialism and was executed by the **oligarchy**, few select members of a single political party, until the breakup of the USSR circa 1992 AD.

During the post 'World War II', (later half of 20th century era), covert ideological cold war raged that pitted Capitalist bloc and 'Socialist or Communist bloc against each other. Each side engaged in no-holds-barred, insidious operations inside and outside its bloc to boost and orchestrate its financial, ideological and political superiority.

NATO

The Capitalist bloc countries, USA, Canada and European countries formed a new military alliance called NATO (North Atlantic Treaty Organization) soon after the 2nd World War. The covert cold war mania climaxed in **'Cuban Missile Crises'** in (1962). Fortunately the sanity on part of the leaderships of both blocs prevailed and averted the smoldering covert cold war flaring into full fledged catastrophic overt nuclear war.

After the breakup of the USSR, the erstwhile communist bloc countries' political leaderships have apparently tempered their political system with relatively more liberal and transparent political ideology.

With the breakup of USSR the political ideologies rivalries between capitalist bloc and old communist bloc apparently subsided. However the smoldering contentious issues tend to flare up occasionally as in Ukraine recently.

Common Wealth

Following the downfall of British Imperialism, circa 1940s, a Britain-led organization called 'Common Wealth', consisting of erstwhile British colonies and extant dominions was formed. The 'Common Wealth' organization doesn't have significant economic, political or diplomatic clout within or outside its members' territories.

Non-aligned bloc

Non-aligned bloc was formed in circa 1960s. It consisted of then recently emancipated (freed) countries after centuries of servitude under European colonial and imperial powers. The non-aligned nations that had begun to put their post-colonial fledgling political and economic houses in order were dubbed as 'developing countries'; or 'Third World'.

Diverse Political Ideologies, Systems

The secular democratic political and justice system rooted in Magna Carta weighs in favour of human and constitutional rights, civil liberties and freedoms. However the political system is prone to political wrangling, prolonged bureaucratic red tape and judicial litigations. The accused is deemed innocent until proven guilty. The onus is on prosecution to prove the guilt.

The autocratic, theocratic and oligarchic political and justice systems weigh in favor of regimes and bureaucracy. The systems are prone to fascism, despotism, kangaroo courts and summary justice.

Evidently all political systems, past and present, have had spells of fascism, tyranny, terror and witch-hunt; unleashed by fascists, ideologues and megalomaniacs.

Megalomaniac Adolf Hitler (1889-1945 AD)

Having failed twice to enter Viennese school of art at the age of eighteen, Adolf Hitler worked as part time construction worker and draftsman. During the World War I (1914 -18 AD) corporal Hitler fought in Germany's Bavarian regiment.

Hitler was jailed for his complicity in 1923 coup. During his eight months' incarceration, he wrote a book, **'Mein Kempf''** 'My Struggle', detailing his early life struggles and bigoted agenda to avenge Germany's World War I defeat for which he blamed the Jews mainly.

While living in Munich, he organized a small nationalist party, Nationalsozalistische Deutsche Arbeiterpartei (National Socialist German Workers party), popularly known as the notorious Nazi Party.

Endowed with sinister charisma, demagogy, polity and dubious organizer, Hitler indoctrinated the post World

War 1, demoralized German people with master-Aryan-race premise and stacked the Nazi Party ranks with indoctrinated master-Aryan-race Germans and built the party into a dominant political force.

Hitler was elected Germany's Chancellor in 1933 AD; and in 1934 he became president and supreme commander of Armed forces i.e. a de facto dictator.

Hitler soon turned out to be a megalomaniac and uncanny tyrant and unleashed bigoted dominant master-Aryan-race agenda and bloody vendetta against Germany's alleged traitors, communists, gypsies, trade unionists, Jews, et al.

Megalomaniac Hitler's quest to create 1000-year 'Third Reich' (3rd mighty Empire) (Ist Roman Empire, 2nd German Empire of Bismarck), started in 1938 AD with the annexation of Austria and Czechoslovakia's border region, Studentland.

War-monger Hitler's invasion of neighboring countries, in 1939 AD triggered World War II, and beginning of the end of Hitler's fascist Nazi regime and 1000-year 'Third Reich. The spectre of 'Third Reich' faded into oblivion in April 1945 AD. Hitler committed suicide on 29 April 1945 along with his wife, Eva Brown whom he had married just a day earlier.

Fascist Joseph Stalin (1879-1953 AD)

Stalin, son of a shoemaker was born in Georgia, Russia and attended a theological seminary in Tiflis. He joined Russian Social Democratic Party and revolutionary movement in late 1890s, and in 1903 he joined **Bolshevik** wing. Stalin was elected member of central committee of the party in 1912 AD. He was jailed often for his revolutionary role.

Stalin rose to the senior position of general secretary of the communist party and built his power base. He succeeded Lenin who died in 1924 AD and ruthlessly expunged opposition, Trotsky, Kamenev, Zinovyev (Zinoviev), et al. By 1927 AD he had established him-self as unrivaled communist party leader and government head.

With purge of party and army in 1930s Stalin assumed absolute control and ruled Russia with iron hand. In 1939 AD Russia and Germany signed non-aggression pact. Hitler reneged and invaded Russia in 1941 AD. The German troops moved at astonishingly brisk pace and reached Leningrad and Stalingrad in November 1941. The Russian counter offensive routed the German invaders and led to eventual downfall of Hitler and 'Third Reich'.

Stalin's ruthless elimination of opposition and implementation of Marxist socialist political ideology, i.e. state controlled communal ownership of property, production and distribution of goods' turned USSR into proverbial secret (KGB) police state, and super power.

In other words authoritarian Stalin forged Soviet Union into communist state, modelled on industrial and agricultural collectivism; and a super power rivalrous to USA. His iron fisted, KGB bolstered secret police state rule and absolute media control earned USSR, **'Iron Curtain'** epithet.

Ideologue Joe McCarthy (1908-57 AD)

American politician Joseph Raymond McCarthy was elected as Republican senator to the US senate from Wisconsin in 1946 AD.

Soon after, his symptoms of deep rooted hatred of communism surfaced. And in 1950 AD he shocked the nation with accusation of 'infiltration of communist spies in the State Department'.

As chairman of Permanent Senate Investigation Sub-committee (1950-54 AD), he pursued covert agenda fraught with communist phobia and witch-hunt. The senate formally censured and ousted him after series of (1953-54 AD) hearings into the unsubstantiated 'subversion of the US Army' allegation. He died in 1957.

Joe McCarthy's unsubstantiated allegations, blacklists, witch-hunts and Machiavellian shenanigans were termed *'McCarthyism'*.

Chapter 5

CONTEMPORARY GLOBAL CONFLICTS

The contemporary Global conflicts are political and religiosity oriented ideological and are of political-religious nature, holocaust proportions.

Partition of Indian Sub-Continent

The partition of Indian Sub-Continent, Jewel of British Colonial Raj, in 1947 was motivated by ultra opportunist leaders, Jawahar Lal Nehru of Indian National Congress party and Mohammad Ali Jinnah of Muslim League Party. The latter, too belonged to Multi-Religious-cultural Indian National Congress Party during its arduous struggle to free India from British Imperialism.

However, the obsession to be supreme leader of independent Indian Sub-Continent set them vying for the highly prestigious position. Mohammad Ali Jinnah, having lost to predominant Hindu element supported Jawahar Lal Nehru, played religious trump card demanding separate Muslim state, Pakistan comprising of majority Muslim population regions.

Despite India's Viceroy, Lord Mountbatten's dissuasion, Mohammad Ali Jinnah remained adamant. Indian Sub-Continent was partitioned into two nations, India and Pakistan, comprising of East Bengal, West Punjab, Sind, North West territories.

The religion driven partition blew open 'Pandora's Box', set off sectarian riots, exoduses and sparked smouldering religious animosities turning men into bestial monsters. Bands of murderous Muslim, Hindu and Sikh thugs committed genocides, carnages and rape. Many young girls and women committed suicides to escape rape, abduction and slavery.

This author, then a juvenile remembers the fateful afternoon when word spread like wild that Muslims hordes were coming to attack. All the Jat-Sikhs of the village packed up bare necessities for the journey to India in matters of hours and left for a nearby village, where Jat-Sikhs of villages were to camp.

I remember, seemingly military truck loads of Muslim soldiers or imposters descending on our transitory camp. All these year I was under the vague impression that the Muslim raiders came for the sole purpose to rob the Jat-Sikh refugees of their valuables. A recurring nightmare now nags me often that they might have raped our women, like Hindus or Sikhs raped their women in India.

At the Pakistan/India border crossing town, Khemkaran, I, the author saw a floating body in a canal. In my ancestral Indian village, I often saw a young, beautiful Muslim girl, kept by a Sikh (Nihang), running screaming unintelligibly. She had gone mad, likely due to heinous atrocity induced trauma.

A pre-partition Muslim village, where we were first settled after exodus from Pakistan, was totally destroyed, not a single house was intact. In all probability band of area Sikhs had ransacked and looted the houses to bare mud walls.

These weren't isolated, instances. Bands of fiends, on both sides of the divide, raided villages and camps, looted, butchered fleeing minority refugees, and abducted their girls and women. Trainloads of butchered children, young, old men and women crossed to and from both sides.

Noble deeds too were done on both sides. The SGPC Secretary, S. Kewal Singh along with few Sikh volunteers did one such deed. They rescued about 30-40

Muslim hapless women from Sikh ruffians who had incarcerated them in an old stable in Amritsar. The rescuers took the Muslim women to Golden Temple complex and lodged them in Guru Ram Das Sarai (tavern) and deployed Sikh women guards for their protection.

The destitute Muslim women were taken care and assured of safe passage to Pakistan. They were taken across the border after 10-12 days and handed over to Pakistani authorities.

Sikh Genocide 1984

Tens of thousands of Sikhs were brutally massacred, their properties looted or vandalized in cities across India by Hindu thugs in Nov. 1084. See **'Target: Sikhism'** p 195

Global Political Religious Mortal Conflict

'The roots of the contemporary mortal conflict between USA-led NATO bloc's coalition of fundamentalist Christians and Judaic Israel alliance Jews vs. Islamic theocratic nations and Jihadist organizations extend way back to the creation of Israel and beyond. The victims of anti-Zionism, the Russian and European Jews had started to return to the Promised Land in early 20th century.

The exodus, in the aftermath of world war II swelled ranks of Jewish population in the modern state of Israel established in 1948 in pursuit of League of Nation's 1922 mandate urging UK to honour its 1919 pledge to facilitate establishment of Jewish 'National Home' given to Jews for helping UK in bringing about the downfall of Ottoman Empire.

The new Jewish 'National home' land irked the Islamic Arab neighbours and Palestinians. They jointly attacked Jewish settlements in 1948. The fledgling Israel militia routed coalition forces of Egypt, Iraq, Jordan, Lebanon and Syria.

The 1948 war broke out when the British commissioner and troops exited Palestine on 14 May and ended on July 17, 1948. The victorious Israelis captured western Galilee, northern Palestine and Lydda, an important Airport city on the strategic Tel Aviv- Jerusalem highway.

In May 1967 Syrian and Egyptian troops; PLO (Palestinian Liberation League) and Arab militants; and Israeli troops mobilized on Israel's borders. The **Six-Day War** started on 5 June 1967. In lightening Air strikes the Israeli fighter planes destroyed Syrian, Egyptian and Jordanian Air forces' planes. And the Israeli Army advanced rapidly into Sinai Peninsula and Syria.

Israel occupied Palestinian territories, including Gaza Strip, Syrian Golan Heights, Egypt's Sinai Peninsula and Jordanian West bank. The Israel has retained control of the occupied territories, except Sinai Peninsula, ever since. The Israel's imperious control of occupied Palestinian territories and building of Jewish settlements there-on, have likely inflamed Jihadists passions of zealous Islamists against Zionists, Jews and allies

The existing Islamic Jihadist organizations became proactive in avenging real or perceived assault on Islam and Muslims. Many more such militant organizations sprouted rapidly, worldwide, some sponsored secretly by Islamic theocracies, autocracies or dictatorships.

The contemporary political and religious conflict has turned exceedingly religious and escalated into mortal combats, pitting Jihadist Islamists against Jew and Christian fundamentalists, especially in US and Israel. Both sides have been launching pre-emptive and retaliatory strikes, guerilla raids or terrorist attacks,

The mortal combat epitomized on September 11, 2001. The radical Islamic terrorists attacked and devastated New York's twin towers with hijacked US Aeroplanes, killing thousands of innocent people including children.

Even before murderous assault by Islamic Jihadist terrorists' on September 11 on New York's twin towers, the fundamentalist evangelicals, zealous Christian Zionists, ultra-orthodox Jews and neoconservatives in US and Israel were making mutual overtures to pursue common cause, to 'counter Islamic threat to Israel; and establish United States government's political hegemony over resource-rich, especially OIL rich Middle East.

The United States has powerful pro-Israel lobbies and advocacy groups including influential Jewish community, Christian Moral Majority, Christian Zionists, ultra-orthodox evangelicals and neoconservative ideologues (neocons).

"So I came to believe that it was in America's best interest to be friends with Israel." **Jerry Falwell**, Fundamentalist Evangelist

'To the Christian evangelicals in America Israel's birth in 1948 was nothing less than the fulfilment of their millennial dreams, (biblical Christ's 1000 year holy and happy reign prophesy). "I consider it the greatest event, from a prophetic standpoint, has taken place... perhaps since 70 A.D. when Jerusalem was destroyed" *(by Romans)'* **Louis Talbot,** Bible institute, Los Angeles.' THE FALL OF THE HOUSE OF BUSH, p. 108

Menachem Begin, militant Zionist, Prime Minister of Israel (1977-83) awarded Jabotinsky prize to evangelical zealot **Jerry Falwell** and gave his ministry a private jet in 1980. Ibid, p. 109

'In 1982, Falwell brought more than three dozen evangelical leaders from moral Majority to Israel to foster ties between Israelites and American evangelicals. He cultivated friendships and political alliances with Menachem Begin, Benjamin and Netanyahu Ariel Sharon. Israel gave multimillion-dollar grants to Falwell's Liberty University, enabling him to bring as many as three thousand students at a time from Liberty University to tour the Holy Land.' Ibid, p. 111

'The International Christian Embassy of Jerusalem, a Christian Zionist organization with no diplomatic standing, set up shop in the holy city with intention of providing evangelical support to Israel. The new travel agencies sponsored Bible Prophesy Tours. Bible tourism soared.' Ibid, p. 111

The rightist political ideologues dubbed as neoconservatives started dabbling in American polity in 1960s. The latter-day neoconservatives, Donald Rumsfeld, Dick Cheney, Paul Wolfowitz, Richard Perle, Lewis 'Scooter' Libby, Zalmay Khalilzad et al, turned out to be ultra rightist ideologues. Dubbed as 'Chickenhawk Groupthink', they occupied senior executive posts in the Republican presidencies. The draft dodgers, Cheney, Wolfowitz, Libby and Khalilzad have held vital Defence Policy Planning, Strategy and resources posts in US Pentagon.

Eventually, neoconservative ideologues, ultra-orthodox evangelicals and zealous Christian Zionists, and American Israel Public Affairs Committee, (AIPAC) coalesced into a loose coalition. Arguably, the common causes, USA's greed for Middle East oil, its hegemony and Israel's survival amid hostile Islamic theocratic and autocratic nations, conjoined Christians and Jews.

Paul Wolfowitz, Under Secretary of Defense, Lewis Scooter Libby and Zalmay Khalilzad, Deputy Under Secretaries of Defense for Strategy and Policy Planning drafted radical 46-page Defense Planning Guidance Paper or document reveals mindset of Neoconservative clique dubbed as 'Chickenhawk Groupthink, The trio piqued by senior George Bush's decision not to pursue regime change and occupy Iraq in the wake of triumphant 'Operation 'Desert Storm' War, wrote,

'America's goal should be to "prevent the emergence of a new rival" to U.S. supremacy as the lone global superpower....In the Middle East and South west Asia, our overall objective is to remain the predominant outside power in the region and preserve U.S. and Western access to region's oil." To achieve America's new objectives, however, Wolfowitz and company decided it was necessary to rewrite the long-standing rules of engagement under which the United States might take military action, employing stratagems that violated the most sacred principles of American policy. THE FALL OF THE HOUSE OF BUSH, p. 116

'Secretary of State James Baker told President Bush (senior) to watch out for the "kooks" working for Cheney.' Ibid, p. 117

"Every ten years or so, the United States needs to pick up some small crappy little country and throw it against the wall, just to show the world we mean business." (Cheney's kook) **Michael Ledeen's** Ibid, p. 149

The radical agenda of the fundamentalist Christian evangelists, Zionists and Chickenhawk Groupthink ideologues' clique was abetted by an Iraqi exile and Jordanian fugitive, **Ahmed Chalabi**, whose father; Abdul

Haydi had served as president of Iraqi senate and a minister in Jordan.

Ahmed Chalabi, with doctorate in mathematics from University of Chicago, where he met Paul Wolfowitz and Richard Perle, moved to Jordan and founded Petra Bank, country's 2nd largest bank. Chalabi family fled Jordan for London in 1989. Jordanian military court found Chalabi guilty of embezzlement, theft, forgery currency speculation and sentenced him in absentia to 22-years hard labour and fined $230 millions.

To the clique of Chickenhawk Groupthink ideologues, Christian fundamentalists and Zionist Jews, Ahmed Chalabi was godsend. The Iraqi exile and Jordanian fugitive with consummate political ambition and personal revenge against rulers of his native lands played a key role in Invasion of Iraq by feeding false information to US war mongers.

Shaha Ali Riza born in Libya, raised in Saudi Arabia and educated in London, working for **'Free Iraq Foundation'** an acolyte and mistress of Jewish Paul Wolfowitz, was another godsend malcontent Arab to the US ideologues' clique, obsessed with regime changes in Middle East.

The' US war mongers' coalition, Christian fundamentalists, neocon ideologues, hard line Jew and Christian Zionist, who had been goading the US administrations to change regimes, impose US hegemony and redraw territorial maps in the Middle East, was strengthened with the addition of malcontent Arabs, Chalabi, Shaha Ali Riza, et al.

The election, in 2000, of President **George W. Bush**, (junior) an explicit critic of his father president Bush (Senior) for not toppling **Sadam Hussein** and occupying Iraq in wake of 1st Gulf War, was dream come true for the war mongers' coalition conspiring invasion of Islamic theocratic and autocratic nations surrounding democratic Israel.

No wonder, since the born again evangelical George W. Bush (Junior) was elected by the shenanigans of the evangelicals and neocons. They secured his victory by mounting election crusade against secular Democrat Al Gore and thwarting recount of close-call vote result in Florida,

The fundamentalist Christians, Jews and neocon ideologues' coalition that elected George W. Bush, deemed him to be a foreign policy moron but an enthusiastic 'Commander-in-Chief' who would readily implement their prejudicial Middle East agenda.

"The first time I met Bush 43 *(43rd US president)*, I knew he was different." "One, he didn't know very much." **Richard Perle**, THE FALL OF THE HOUSE OF BUSH, p 166

"His *(Bush 43)* ignorance of the world cannot be overstated". US state department source, Ibid p 166

'Then *(Paul)* **Wolfowitz** and *(Condoleeza)* **Rice** started going down to Austin *(Texas)* to tutor Bush in foreign policy, …' Ibid p 166

Tutoring of Paul Wolfowitz and Condoleeza merely hyped resolve of uncanny George W Bush, who had said, "He was an instrument of God;" *(to invade Iraq?)*.

The rationalist politicians, and journalists cautioned, and the anti-war groups protested against the looming Iraq Invasion.

'Well aware that *(Iraq)* war was afoot, *(Brent)* Scowcroft had tried to head it off with an August 15, 2002, Wall Street Journal op-ed piece titled "Don't attack

Sadam.... There is scant evidence to tie Sadam to terrorism," he wrote, "and even less to Sept. 11 attacks" To attack Iraq, while ignoring the Israeli-Palestinian conflict, he said, "could turn whole region into cauldron and thus destroy the war on terrorism." THE FALL OF the HOUSE OF BUSH P. 5

'She *(FBI agent **Coleen Rowley**)* wrote to (Bob) Mueller eight months earlier, in *(circa* March, *2003)* warning that the coming war was a distraction from the country's real focus on ,terrorism and would "bring an exceptional increase in the terrorist threat to the US, both at home and abroad". BUSH'S LAW, THE REMAKING OF AMERICAN JUSTICE, p. 123

'Did that mean *(FBI)* agents should begin poking around into activities of a group that angrily accused Bush of being a war criminal, or Cheney of being a war-profiteering criminal?' Ibid, p 123

(President) "Bush (junior) and *(John)* Ashcroft were casting the struggle against terrorism as one of good versus evil, a global clash of cultures depicted in often starkly religious terms." Ibid, p 60

Evidently, the USA-led 2003 Operation Iraq Liberation was not launched for the purported reasons, i.e. Iraq's cache of Weapons of Mass Destruction and Sadam Hussein's support of Islamic terrorists. No Weapons of Mass Destruction cache or link to terrorists was found.

President George W. Bush and his underlings' were motivated to invade Iraq by prejudicial agenda to impose USA's strategic hegemony in Middle East and ulterior motive, to secure unimpeded access to Iraq's oil.

Dick Cheney, President Ford's chief of staff rankled by the oil price hike by OPEC in 1973, had been lobbying Western Allies and conspiring, ever since to expropriate control of Middle East oil.

"By 2010 we will need on the order of an additional fifty million barrels *(of oil)* a day, he said in a speech before the London Institute of Petroleum in 1999, when he was CEO of **Halliburton,** the giant energy services company. "So where is the oil going to come from? ... the Middle East with two third of the world's oil and lowest cost, is still the prize ultimately". THE FALL OF the HOUSE OF BUSH, p 202

'Cheney knew, given America's close relationship with Saudi Arabia, world's biggest oil producer, that a new, friendly pro-West regime in Iraq, with someone like Chalabi in charge would put the United States in a much stronger position with respect to OPEC.' Ibid, p 202

The disingenuous neocon ideologues, Dick Cheney, and his underlings, who occupied key posts in neophyte president George W. Bush's administration, had more ulterior motives than 'Operation Iraq Liberation' ruse.

'..., if the United States overthrow Sadam Hussein and liberated the Shi'ites, far more than just greeting Americans with flowers, the Shi'ites would also take on the Islamic state of Iran. Democracy would spread throughout the region *(Middle East)*! Israel would be secure and the U.S. would have allies in oil-rich states of Iran and Iraq.' **Paul Wolfowitz,** Ibid, p. 149

'.... on January 30, 2001, at the administration's first National Security Council (NSC).... When the president *(George W. Bush)* opened his mouth, it was as if he were channeling Wolfowitz. As far as the Middle East was concerned, the new administration was listening to the neocons *(war mongers)*, not Richard Clark *(destroy Al-Qaeda advocate)*. "We're going to correct the imbalance of the previous administration on the Middle East conflict." Bush announced, "We're going to tilt it back toward Israel."

'On February 1, 2001, two days after NSC *(National Security Council)* meeting Bush officials circulated a memo titled "Plan for post Saddam Iraq" and began discussing what to do with Iraq's oil wealth'. THE FALL OF THE HOUSE *of* BUSH, p. 202

While the USA-led NATO intervention in Afghanistan to dislodge (US and Pakistan created monster), 'holy terror' 'Taliban' from theocratic seat of power, is laudable, same cannot be said of the intervention in Middle East on false pretense 'to usher in democracy.

In retrospection, the US-led invasion of Iraq opened up proverbial 'Pandora's Box'. The US economy suffered setback and approval rating of leader of the US war mongers pack, George W. Bush dropped to lowest ever for an outgoing US president.

Iraqi people were terrorized; hundreds of thousands were killed and prisoners were tortured and humiliated during 'Operation Iraq Liberation'. Deadly power struggle; ethnic cleansing, genocides and sectarian bloodshed erupted after OIL fiasco.

Evidently, pogroms unleashed in wake of US-led 'Operation Iraq Liberation' overshadow atrocities perpetrated in Middle East before OIL subterfuge. The radical Islamic rebels have unleashed carnage, pogroms and genocide to carve an authoritarian theocratic Islamic state out of swaths of bordering Iraqi and Syrian territories.

Contrary to US war mongers" Middle East pretense, 'to eliminate threat posed by Iraqi dictator

Sadam Hussein's support of Islamic terrorists and Weapons of Mass Destruction, the militant Jihadists have converged in Middle East and turned the region into anarchic inferno. However the OIL fiasco did accomplish US war mongers' portentous motive *'turn Palestinian-Israeli conflict imbalance in Israel's favour'*.

While despotism, fascism, tyranny, summary justice and punishments are rampant in autocratic, theocratic oligarchic and dictatorial regimes, any attempt to change the status quo, turns the law and order situation worse. With the strongman; dictator or autocrat disposed of any semblance of law and order breaks down. The bloody power struggle, civil or sectarian war and ethnic cleansing ensue. The murderous sectarian and ethnic Militias turn country into combative killing zones.

The USA led Operation Iraq Liberation', OIL popularly perceived to be quest for Iraqi oil, Coup d'é tat in Libya and Egypt; and bloody power struggle in Syria exemplify the pogroms, carnage and rampage that ensue attempted status quo change or regime change.

Unfortunately, it's the innocent peoples who bear the brunt of upheavals; death, destruction, rape, exodus, etc. The inciters, instigators and war mongers reap the benefits or fade into oblivion.

While the 'Operation Iraq Liberation' (OIL) subterfuge victims suffer the Islamic Jihadists' vengeance, the OIL protagonists, George W. Bush, Dick Cheney, Donald Rumsfeld, Paul Wolfowitz, Richard Perle, Lewis 'Scooter' Libby, Zalmay Khalilzad, Condoleezza Rice; and malcontent Arabs Ahmad Chalabi Shaha Ali Riza, Curveball (code name) et al, have disappeared into oblivion.

The OIL subterfuge has not only abetted the radicalization of the Jihadists of Islamic theocratic and autocratic Nations but also drawn malcontent Christian converts from democratic Western nations to Islamic terrorist organizations. The latter are apparently more ruthless than the former Jihadist terrorists.

The gruesome beheading of two Western correspondents by a ruthless executioner with British accent; and the radical Islamic rebels'' bloody insurgency to carve an authoritarian theocratic Islamic State out of bordering Iraqi and Syrian territories has drawn the US led NATO allies back into the region.

The bloody insurrection of Islamic State carvers has turned the region into hotbed of Jihadist terrorists threatening global peace and security. The turmoil has made strange bed fellows and brought past antagonists, NATO Allies and Arab nations together to confront ominous global threat.

EPILOGUE

Dispensation

Having failed to effectively enforce prohibition of the illicit drug trade, use and/or abuse, some Western jurisdictional authorities, have relaxed or legalized production, possession and dispensing of drugs. The homosexuality exponents and proponents have successfully lobbied for equal rights and benefits available to traditional heterosexuality till recently. The author lacks credentials and qualifications to make judgement calls on dispensation granted to drug cultures and equal rights granted to homosexuals.

Premonition

The ominous predictions and dire projections of cataclysmic storms, floods, droughts; chronic, terminal diseases causing Air pollution; dwindling arable land and non-renewable resources, shortages of life sustaining basic necessities, water food are disconcerting. And scientific studies and reports attributing proliferation of HIV/AIDS, venereal or STDs (sexually transmitted diseases), Meningoencephlitis, syphilis, etc to drug culture and sexual promiscuity, homosexuality and bisexuality exacerbate the premonition that it may, sadly, be nature's grievous way of culling the burgeoning human population, to restore congenial global ecology and environment; and prolong non-renewable resources and ecosystem sustainability.

Postulation

Whether the teeming human population, that surpassed earth's optimal carrying capacity half a century ago, or cyclical natural phenomena; or both are tampering with the global ecosystem and climate is a moot question (debatable). While the mankind cannot control nature, it can control human population to commensurate with optimal carrying capacity of earth.

Supplication

We can only supplicate and hope that the divine nature doesn't resort to apocalyptic means but would devise a merciful means to restore harmonious ecology, essential resources sustainability, environmental clemency and socio-cultural and political congeniality.

Glimmer of Optimism

While the author's treatise 'Contemporary Trends' portrays dismal ecological and environmental picture, there is glimmer of optimism as the mankind has, seemingly, been made conscious of the dire consequences of its reckless trends and tendencies; and impelled it to make amends to worsening environmental and ecological phenomena; and tone down political ideological hostilities and polarizations.

Geopolitical Reconciliations

The process of geopolitical reconciliations started with unification of Germany, bifurcated in the aftermath of 'World War II'; followed by cessation of intensive ideological hostilities, (cold War) between capitalist nations and communist bloc nations in the Korean and Vietnam Peninsulas. It continues with the recent conciliatory overtures between Mainland China and Taiwan; and North and South Korea.

Ecology, Environment, Resource Management

On the ecology and environment fronts global powers are grappling with runaway fossil fuel combustion pollution and Green House Gas emissions. Though belated, efforts are underway to find alternative renewable energy sources and wean mankind from 'Fossil Fuel' energy sources.

The national and provincial governments are setting stringent rules and regulations to regulate fossil fuel extraction, refining and combustion processes and are giving incentives to entrepreneurs to tap into less polluting, renewable energy sources, globally.

The UN Secretary General, Ban Ki-moon in an unprecedented move has appointed New York's former mayor, Mr. Michael Bloomberg to United Nations special climate change envoy *(position)*, mandated to work for humanity and help countries and cities around the world to address the climate change phenomenon.

The global society at large; national, provincial, local municipal leaders and peoples are making concerted efforts to reduce, reuse and recycle consumer goods, packaging and waste materials.

Innovation

The loss of agricultural and horticultural land to mankind's usage; habitat, amenities, facilities and infrastructure, has driven urbanites and suburbanites to innovate and grow food and flowers in residential yards, conservatories and public parks; and on commercial and industrial buildings' rooftops.

Bibliography

Reader's Encyclopedia, Benét's Third Edition

Multimedia Broadcast & published Documentaries, Reports and Studies

Funk & Wagnall's New Encyclopedia

Collin's Discovery Encyclopedia

Wikipedia; Published Papers, Articles

THE FALL OF THE HOUSE *of* BUSH

BUSH'S LAW THE REMAKING OF AMERICAN JUSTICE

AUTHOR'S OTHER WORKS

PUNJABI

1) Akhouti Granthan Di Perdchol;

2) Sikh-Asikhi;

3) Guru Granth, Samperdai Guru, Guru Ghantal

ENGLISH

1) Sikhism anti-Sikhism

2) Target Sikhism

3) Holy Terror, Unholy Tyranny